What I Saw in Yellowstone

Text by Durrae Johanek   Photographs by Christopher Cauble

The Exploration of

_____

(Explorer, A.K.A. your name here)

__/__/__ to __/__/__

(Dates of exploration)

RIVERBEND
PUBLISHING

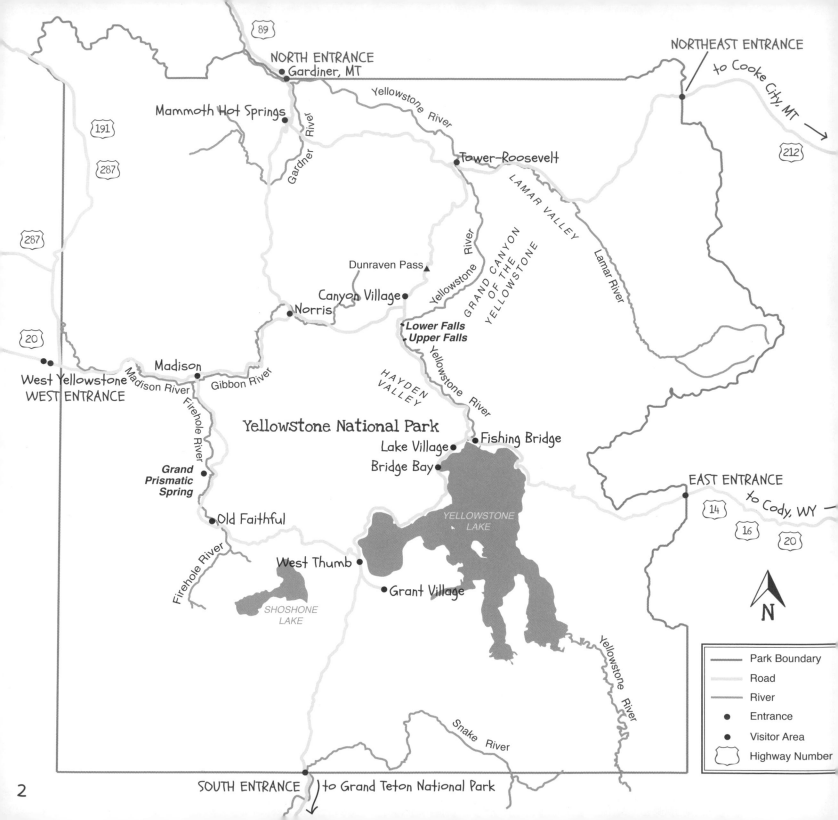

89

NORTH ENTRANCE
Gardiner, MT

NORTHEAST ENTRANCE
to Cooke City, MT

Mammoth Hot Springs

191

287

287

20

West Yellowstone
WEST ENTRANCE

Gardner River

212

Tower-Roosevelt

LAMAR VALLEY

Lamar River

Dunraven Pass

Yellowstone River

Canyon Village

Norris

Lower Falls
Upper Falls

GRAND CANYON OF THE YELLOWSTONE

Madison

Madison River

Gibbon River

Firehole River

HAYDEN VALLEY

Yellowstone River

Yellowstone National Park

Grand
Prismatic
Spring

Old Faithful

Fishing Bridge
Lake Village
Bridge Bay

EAST ENTRANCE
to Cody, WY

14

16

20

YELLOWSTONE LAKE

Firehole River

West Thumb

Grant Village

SHOSHONE LAKE

Yellowstone River

Snake River

N

SOUTH ENTRANCE to Grand Teton National Park

Park Boundary
Road
River
● Entrance
● Visitor Area
Highway Number

Contents

Introduction

Aspen leaf

People have lived in what we now call Yellowstone National Park for thousands of years. Indians were using the area when mountain men (fur trappers) traveled through it in the early to mid-1800s. Some of these men returned to civilization with fantastic stories of bubbling grounds and hot water shooting into the air, but most people didn't believe them. That changed as explorers probed the area, especially after 1871 when Ferdinand Hayden led the third government-sponsored expedition into the Yellowstone country. To prove his findings, he took along William Henry Jackson to photograph the sights, and just in case the photos didn't turn out, he included Thomas Moran, an artist. Between photos and paintings the group had enough evidence of Yellowstone's wonders to approach Congress and suggest this land become a national park. In 1872, it did, becoming the first national park in the world.

Yellowstone's official, and very appropriate, nickname is "Wonderland," and

Fireweed

Gray wolf

visitors come by the millions every year to see this land of wonders. Most stay only a day or two. Some explore every possible corner of the park, and a few are so awed by Yellowstone, they move to Wyoming, Montana, or Idaho, just to be close to it.

More than in any one place on earth, Yellowstone's 2.2 million acres offer Native American history, local and western history, wildlife galore, geysers and hot springs, waterfalls, spectacular scenery, hiking and skiing trails, and at certain times of year, solitude.

What I Saw in Yellowstone will help you find and identify the park's most frequently seen plants, animals, geothermal features, and more, whether you're driving park roads, resting at pull-offs, or hiking. But one major caution: Yellowstone is not an amusement park or a zoo. What you see here is real and can hurt you if you don't use common sense and obey park rules.

Of course *What I Saw in Yellowstone* can't possibly cover everything you'll see—that would take volumes and volumes. For example, great horned and great gray owls live here, but because they're mostly nocturnal (active at night) you're not likely to see them. Some mammals are so uncommon, like the wolverine, that they haven't made the book either.

Male bighorn sheep

But this book has plenty of things to look for. See how many items you can check off, and let your parents help so you can all learn such things as:

Bald eagle

★ More than half of the geysers in the world are in Yellowstone. There are more than 10,000 hydro-thermal features, including 300-plus geysers, in the park.

★ Canyon Visitor Education Center has exhibits on Yellowstone's caldera, the supervolcano, and a mysterious kugel ball.

★ The Old Faithful Visitor Education Center, which opened in 2010, is one of the greenest (environmentally friendly) centers in the country. It has terrific interactive, hands-on exhibits on sustainability and park features.

If you see a plant or animal you can't identify, take a photo and show it to a park ranger, who will do his or her best to help you. If you stump the ranger, go to any of the Yellowstone Association sites (located in most visitor centers) or concessionaires' stores, where you'll find hundreds of books (some in foreign languages) on Yellowstone and everything connected to it.

To have a safe trip through Yellowstone, there are some "do's and don'ts" that you should pay careful attention to:

Little sunflower

★ Don't feed *any* wildlife: It's dangerous to you and certainly not good for the animal.

★ Don't ever throw anything into a geyser, thermal pool, or hot spring—you will damage it.

★ Don't step on thermal features—stay on paths and boardwalks. People have died from falling into boiling waters.

★ Do keep your distance: That huge awkward-looking bison can outrun you. Park rules state that you need to stay 100 yards (that's a football field) away from bears and wolves, and 25 yards away from all other large animals.

★ Do take lots of photos, explore the trails and geyser basins, read the interpretive signs, stop at the visitor centers—and have fun.

America's Wonderland has it all—history, geysers, mud pots, bears, wolves, and now you. Welcome to Yellowstone!

Morning Glory Pool in Upper Geyser Basin

Bison

(Bos bison)

Bison are one of the great wildlife symbols of Yellowstone National Park, and they are easy to see from the roads. You might see them wandering through human areas, but don't approach them because they can be dangerous. In fact, more park visitors have been hurt by bison than any other animal, including grizzly bears.

Bison are often called buffalo, although scientifically speaking, true buffalo and bison are not the same. But if you call a bison a buffalo, everyone will know what you mean.

Male bison are called bulls, females are cows, and their young are calves. Both males and females have thick horns, and they have long, dense hair on their heads and shoulders. The reddish brown calves are born in April and May; as they get older they become dark brown like their parents.

Full-grown bison can be 6 feet tall at the top of their shoulders. You might think such a large animal would be slow, but they are quick when they need to be and can run 30 miles per hour, much faster than a person can run.

Bison are grazers and prefer grasses and similar plants. In winter, they swing their shaggy heads back and forth to sweep away snow so they can reach the grass beneath it.

In any one year, Yellowstone has

A bison shedding its thick winter hair

about 2,000 to 4,000 bison. Their only major predators are wolves and sometimes grizzly bears, and during Yellowstone's harsh winters some bison may starve to death.

Huge herds of bison used to roam the plains of North America, but they were nearly killed to extinction for their hides. A few remained in Yellowstone, which today is one of the few places where you can see them living wild and free.

Guess What?
The bison is the largest animal in North America. A full-grown male can weigh 2,000 pounds—that's a ton!

6   Bison calf

☐ I saw bison!

Where?

When?

How many?

What were they doing?

Elk

(Cervus elaphus)

Where to see them

In summer, throughout the park, especially in high meadows. Look in the **Gibbon River** meadows, in **Hayden Valley**, and along **Dunraven Pass**. **Madison Junction**, the **Firehole River** area, and the **Lamar Valley** are good too, especially in the fall. The community of **Mammoth** has elk around most of the year.

In the fall you might hear an elk before you see it. The male (bull) elk "bugles"—makes a loud call during the mating season—primarily to challenge other males but also to let females (cows) know he's available for breeding. The bugle starts low and rises until it ends in a long, high-pitched squeal, often followed by several loud grunts.

Bull elk bugling

Bull elk grow antlers, which they shed each year. New antlers grow in the spring and summer and are covered with a nourishing membrane called "velvet." When the antlers finish growing in late summer, the velvet dies and is scraped off, leaving the hard antler.

A large set (pair) of elk antlers can be 5 feet wide by 5 feet long and weigh 30 to 40 pounds. That's like carrying a heavy backpack on your head, but for a big bull elk standing nearly 5 feet tall and weighing up to 1,000 pounds, it doesn't seem to be a problem. Yearling bull elk usually just have two straight points for antlers, so these young bulls are commonly called "spikes." Cow elk don't have antlers.

Elk live in herds. In the summer the biggest bulls often form small herds of their own, while the larger herds are made up of cows and young elk. In the fall, all the elk are together. They like to feed in meadows, but they will go into forests to rest, hide, or take shelter from bad weather.

In the spring, a cow elk usually gives birth to one calf. Like deer fawns, elk calves have light spots on their brown fur that make them harder to see when they are lying very still. This helps them hide from predators. As they get older, the spots disappear.

Guess what?

Another name for elk is a Native American (Shawnee) word—wapiti, pronounced WOP-uh-tee. It means "white rump," and when you see elk you'll know why it's a good name for them.

Cow elk crossing Gardner River

☐ **I saw elk!**

Where?

When?

How many?

What were they doing?

9

Deer

Where to see them

Lake, Tower, **Mammoth**, and the shoreline of **Yellowstone Lake** are particularly good areas for mule deer, but they could be seen just about anywhere. White-tailed deer may be seen around Gardiner, Tower, and sometimes in the **Lamar Valley**.

(Odocoileus virginianus) and (Odocoileus hemionus)

Two species of deer live in Yellowstone National Park: white-tailed deer and mule deer. Mule deer are much more common and can be seen throughout the park. White-tailed deer generally remain in lower elevations.

Mule deer doe

When it runs, a whitetail raises its broad tail high, showing the tail's all-white underside like a waving white flag. Mule deer have short tails with black tips, and when they run, they tend to jump from place to place with all four legs springing up and down at the same time, like a four-legged pogo stick: *boing-boing-boing.* This unusual gait is called "stotting" and is used to evade predators. In Yellowstone, deer have to be alert for many predators, especially mountain lions.

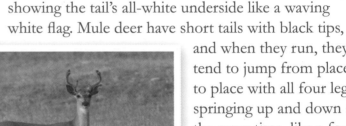

White-tailed deer buck

Mule deer are so named because their large ears resemble the ears of a mule. "Muleys," as they are sometimes called, are larger than white-tailed deer, and their antlers show one or more distinctive "forks" where two antler points grow apart from each other. A whitetail's antlers are a series of individual points from a main beam, and they are rarely forked.

Guess What?

There is a difference between antlers and horns. Antlers are shed each year, but horns stay on and grow throughout an animal's life. Elk, deer, and moose have antlers; bison and bighorn sheep have horns.

☐ I saw mule deer!
☐ I saw white-tailed deer!

Where?

When?

How many?

What were they doing?

Bighorn Sheep

(Ovis canadensis)

Bighorn sheep are about the size of deer, and the first thing you notice about them is their horns. Both male (rams) and female sheep (ewes) have horns but the rams' horns are much larger. A 6- or 7-year-old ram has thick, heavy horns that curve around in a circle. Ewes have short, thin horns that only slightly curve. The horns are made of material similar to your fingernails, and they grow larger, year after year.

Bighorn sheep don't have woolly coats like domestic sheep on farms and ranches. Instead, they have thick hair that helps keep them warm in winter and cool in summer.

Bighorn sheep are some of the most surefooted animals in Yellowstone National Park,

female

young male

and they always live on and near steep cliffs to avoid predators. They have special hooves that help them keep their grip on narrow ledges and slick rocks, even when they jump from one tiny ledge to another.

If you're in Yellowstone in the fall, you may see two rams challenge each other for territory. They charge each other and slam their horns together so hard that the impact makes a loud, sharp "*crack*" sound that can be heard a mile away. Fortunately, their thick skulls protect their brains.

Young sheep, called lambs, are born in the spring and by fall are prancing all over the hillsides, playing and butting heads as they've seen their parents do.

☐ I saw bighorn sheep!

Where?

When?

How many?

What were they doing?

Guess What?

Long ago, a tribe of Native Americans, the Sheepeaters, lived in the Yellowstone area and made their bows from the horns of bighorn sheep.

male

Coyote

(Canis latrans)

Where to see them

Throughout the park in open areas and meadows, especially **Lamar Valley**, the **Tower Junction** area, **Hayden Valley,** Norris Geyser Basin, and Upper Geyser Basin (where Old Faithful is).

Coyotes were the "top dogs" in Yellowstone National Park until wolves were reintroduced in 1995. Now wolves are the top dogs, but coyotes are still here and still frequently seen. In fact, this is an example of how adaptable coyotes are. In Yellowstone they have learned—once again—how to share the landscape with wolves.

An adult coyote is about as tall as a medium-sized dog and weighs about 25-35 pounds. Wolves are much taller and weigh more than twice as much. In Yellowstone, coyotes usually have grayish brown coats (without distinct markings) and big bushy tails.

Coyotes usually avoid wolves because wolves may attack and kill them. But coyotes like to eat the same things wolves eat, and coyotes will frequently sneak around carcasses of animals that wolves have killed, hoping to dash in and grab a bite to eat without being caught. Mostly though, coyotes hunt alone for voles, mice, ground squirrels, rabbits, and other small animals.

Coyotes are very vocal. They bark, yip, yowl, and howl. A rapid series of quickly changing, high-pitched yips is very common, especially around sunrise and sunset. This sound is much different than a wolf's long, deep, steady howl.

In the spring, coyote mothers give birth to pups in ground dens. A litter is usually four or more pups, and the parents bring food to them until the pups are big enough to travel with the parents.

Guess What?

You may pronounce this animal's name as a three-syllable word, kye-O-tee, or two syllables, KYE-ote. Most people in the Yellowstone area say KYE-ote or KYE-yote.

☐ I saw a coyote!

Where?

When?

What was it doing?

Where to see them

Lamar Valley, Slough Creek, **Hayden Valley**, the **Firehole** area, and other places. Ask at a visitor center for recent sightings, and keep your eyes open—wolves can appear just about anywhere.

Gray Wolf

(Canis lupus)

The reintroduction of wolves to Yellowstone is one of the great success stories of modern conservation.

In the early days of the West, wolves were common, but over the years, both inside and outside the park, wolves were hunted and trapped until they were gone. Later, scientists began to learn more about wolves and their role in ecosystems. At the same time, wildlife biologists realized that Yellowstone National Park still had all of its original animal species except for wolves, so in 1995, wildlife officials released a few gray wolves from Canada into the park. A few more wolves were released in 1996. The wolves quickly settled in, and today the park has a good population of wild wolves.

One of the great surprises of returning wolves to Yellowstone is that the animals are seen fairly often—at least compared to other wolf areas in the world. Of course, to have your very best chance of seeing wolves, you need to get up at dawn and look in big open areas with binoculars and spotting scopes.

Wolves live in family groups called packs. A wolf pack is led by "alpha wolves," a male and a female.

The pack mainly preys on large animals such as elk, deer, and sometimes bison, but smaller animals are also eaten. A wolf kill provides food for many other animals. At a fresh kill, ravens, eagles, and magpies usually arrive first, then coyotes (wolves' smaller cousins), and often bears.

You might not see a wolf, but you might hear wolves howling, and that is a great experience too.

Guess What?
A wolf's howl can be heard from a mile away.

☐ I saw wolves!

Where?

When?

How many?

What were they doing?

Black Bear

(Ursus americanus)

Where to see them

The **Antelope Creek** area between Tower Falls and Mount Washburn, the **Lamar** and **Hayden valleys**, in meadows between Mammoth and Tower.

About 1,000 black bears live in Yellowstone National Park. Watch for them on hillsides, in meadows, and even in trees, which they sometimes climb to avoid danger. As you drive through the park, be alert for a bunch of cars stopped along the road. It could be a "bear jam" where many people have stopped to look at a bear.

Black bears share Yellowstone with grizzly bears, but they are almost never found together. Grizzly bears are bigger and more powerful than black bears and sometimes attack black bears, so black bears usually stay away from them.

To tell a black bear from a grizzly bear, look for rumps and humps. When standing on all four feet, a black bear's rump is a little taller than its front shoulders, but a grizzly bear's rump is lower than the big hump on its front shoulders.

Black bears eat mostly plants and you will probably see them cracking open logs, looking for grubs and insects, or eating berries, but when they can get it, they also eat meat, including trout and elk calves. They even eat ants and bees!

Black bears are active from spring through fall, but in the winter, they enter dens and go to sleep—a very deep sleep. They sometimes wake up, and females give birth to cubs in the dens, but they mostly sleep through the winter until spring comes.

Guess What?

Not all black bears are black: their hair color varies from almost blond to cinnamon to brown to dark black.

☐ I saw a black bear!

Where?

When?

What was it doing?

14

Where to see them

Some of the best places to find grizzlies are the expansive meadows that are visible from the road between Canyon Village and Tower Junction, especially the **Antelope Creek Bear Management Area** just north of **Dunraven Pass**. Other good places are **Hayden Valley**, the forest and meadow area between **Hayden Valley** and **Fishing Bridge**, the meadows between **Mammoth** and **Norris**, and between **Yellowstone Lake** and the park's east entrance.

Grizzly Bear

(Ursus arctos)

The grizzly bear is one of the most looked-for animals in Yellowstone, but it is not easy to see. You might be lucky and see one from a park road during the middle of the day, but if you really want to see a grizzly, you should get up at dawn and look in vast meadows of grass and sagebrush where the bears forage for food. But stay on the road and use binoculars to look for them.

Grizzly bears are larger than black bears. A male grizzly (called a boar) can weigh as much as 850 pounds and be about 3 ½ feet tall at the shoulder when it is standing on all four feet, and much taller when it stands on its two hind legs to get a better look at something. Grizzlies have cubs every three or four years. When born, the cubs weigh about one pound, but they grow quickly. They stay with the mother bear for two to three years until they're almost as big as she is.

A "griz" goes into a deep sleep in winter, and comes out of its den in spring to dig for roots, bulbs, and grubs. But it is omnivorous (eats plants and animals) and will just as eagerly feed on an animal carcass.

Wolves and grizzlies have an interesting relationship. Wolves may try to kill grizzly cubs, but grizzlies benefit from wolves by feeding on carcasses of animals that wolves have killed.

☐ I saw a grizzly bear!

Where?

When?

What was it doing?

Guess What?

The grizzly bear is sometimes called "silvertip" because the tips of its long hairs are light-colored or silvery, especially on older bears. Another word for this coloration is "grizzled," which gives us the name, "grizzly."

Red Squirrel

(Tamiasciurus hudsonicus)

If you get too close to a red squirrel you'll know it because it chatters loudly and lets out a squirrel yell that's hard to ignore. It lives in forests and is very territorial (it doesn't like other squirrels in its area). Not only will it chase other squirrels that come too close, it will chatter at any intruder, including you.

Red squirrels are really rust colored, not bright red, and they are smaller than gray squirrels and fox squirrels common in other places.

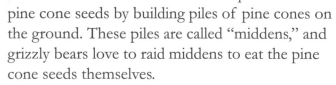

One habit of red squirrels is very important for Yellowstone's grizzly bears. Red squirrels store pine cone seeds by building piles of pine cones on the ground. These piles are called "middens," and grizzly bears love to raid middens to eat the pine cone seeds themselves.

Guess What?

The little red squirrel and the big grizzly bear share a common food—pine cone seeds.

Uinta ground squirrels hibernate for about seven months—that's most of the year!

Where to See them

You can see red squirrels in forests throughout the park, especially around **Old Faithful**, **Canyon**, and park campgrounds. You can see ground squirrels in sagebrush meadows and around **Mammoth Hot Springs**, **Old Faithful**, and **Canyon Village**.

Ground Squirrel

(Urocitellus armatus)

Ground squirrels are common in Yellowstone National Park's grass and sagebrush meadows—and around human areas. They are easy to recognize: if that brownish, furry-tailed little animal scampering across the road or standing on a dirt mound in a meadow is bigger than a chipmunk, then it's a Uinta ground squirrel. They create underground burrows, often with more than one opening or "door," usually marked by a low mound of bare dirt.

Ground squirrels are a great food source for many predators such as coyotes, foxes, and badgers, and for raptors (birds of prey) such as hawks and eagles. Even grizzly bears dig for ground squirrels.

☐ **I saw a red Squirrel!**
☐ **I saw a ground Squirrel!**

Where?

When?

What was it doing?

16

Marmot

(Marmota flaviventris)

The yellow-bellied marmot is correctly named—it has a yellow-gold belly that is visible when it stands on its hind legs, which it does a lot, watching for danger such as eagles and coyotes.

In the western United States, marmots are also called rock chucks because rocks are where they live. The rocks make it almost impossible for a predator to dig them out. But marmots have to venture into meadows to feed on their favorite plant foods.

Don't confuse marmots and ground squirrels. Marmots are much bigger, have darker fur, and their tails are bushier. Marmots also like to sun themselves on rocks.

Marmots hibernate most of the year, from late summer until spring.

☐ **I saw a marmot!**
☐ **I saw a chipmunk!**

Where?

When?

What was it doing?

Where to see them

You can see chipmunks in the **Old Faithful** area, in campgrounds, picnic areas, and along trails. You can see marmots on rocky slopes and large stone piles throughout the park, for example, Sheepeater Cliffs. **Mount Washburn** is another good spot, and you might even see one hanging around the boardwalks at **Old Faithful**.

Chipmunk

(Tamias species)

Chipmunks are some of the most commonly seen little animals in Yellowstone.

You might see one run across a road or scamper along a trail. You will probably see them in human areas such as campgrounds, picnic areas, and popular places like Old Faithful. Chipmunks are curious and will approach people, but don't try to touch them or feed them—human food is never meant for wildlife.

Chipmunks are small members of the squirrel family. They are reddish brown with long bushy tails and thin white stripes on the back and face.

Chipmunks hardly ever sit still unless they pause to eat something. They eat seeds and nuts that they gather and store for the winter, and they eat small insects. They also get eaten by larger animals and birds of prey.

Guess what?

When alarmed, the chipmunk gives a sharp call that sounds like *chip*—a good bet that's how it got its name.

If you are hiking in high, rocky areas and hear someone whistling at you, look around for a marmot. Their warning call is a loud, high-pitched whistle.

17

Common Raven

Where to see them

Old Faithful, **Fishing Bridge**, the **Grand Canyon of the Yellowstone**, and any place that attracts people.

(Corvus corax)

Ravens are all black, like crows, but bigger. A raven also has a thicker bill, a wedge-shaped tail (visible when flying), and makes different sounds. In fact, ravens makes lots of different sounds. Their call is loud and hoarse, written as *cawkk, cawkk, cawkk* or *awwkk, awwkk, awwkk*. It's deeper and a little longer than a crow's *caw, caw*. Another common call in flight is a two-note *kloo-klak*. You may also hear a high, rapid, knocking sound, *doc-doc-doc*. Ravens make softer sounds, too, like *quork-ing,* and they even mimic sounds they hear, like water gurgling.

Ravens are common in all habitats in Yellowstone National Park. You'll see ravens around Old Faithful, Canyon, and most places where there are humans— and human food that ravens try to find. Of course, don't feed them. Ravens are quite capable of finding natural food such as insects, seeds, and berries, and they are excellent hunters, sometimes swooping low to pick mice off the ground. They especially like to feed on dead animals. In the winter there may be dozens of ravens around the carcass of an animal killed by wolves, just waiting for a chance to grab a piece of meat from the carcass.

Like other members of the crow family, ravens are smart, especially when it comes to finding food. In Yellowstone, ravens have learned how to open people's unattended backpacks, even some packs with zippers, to get food inside.

Guess What?

Yellowstone is too high in elevation for vultures, so here, ravens and eagles fill the role of vultures by eating animal carcasses, with help from magpies.

☐ I saw a raven!

Where?

When?

What was it doing?

Black-billed Magpie

(Pica hudsonia)

There's no mistaking this bird for any other in Yellowstone National Park. It is vividly black and white, has a very long tail—nearly a foot long, about as long as its body—and is fairly large, almost as large as a crow, a close relative.

☐ I saw a magpie!

Where?

When?

What was it doing?

The black-billed magpie lives in open country and eats just about anything: seeds, nuts, berries, carrion (animal carcasses), and even other birds. It's often seen at a carcass, competing with other birds and animals for a piece of meat. Sometimes a magpie will land on the back or head of a live bison or elk and eat insects on the animal, especially ticks.

Magpies are abundant in the West and can be seen in open country at lower elevations, or wherever there is carrion to feed on. They can also be found in forests and mountain areas.

One sign of magpies is a large, bulky nest made of sticks, usually in a tall tree next to open areas. Some nests are very big; they have been used year after year, with more sticks added every year.

The nest is a good home for the four or five baby magpies born in the spring. Little by little as they grow bigger, they work their way out of the nest, calling and begging for food. In fact, magpies and their young can be quite noisy, squawking to each other. Young magpies look just like their parents except they have short, stubby tails. It takes them a couple of months to grow their long tails.

Guess what?

Magpies often "cache" or hide pieces of food to eat later, but if other magpies are watching, a magpie may make several false caches before making a real one, trying to fool the others so they can't find the food.

19

Osprey

(Pandion haliaetus)

Ospreys are seen along Yellowstone National Park's rivers and lakes, flying above the water, perched on waterside trees and cliffs, or sitting in their nests.

Ospreys hunt fish, spotting them from the air. Sometimes an osprey will hover briefly in one place, watching and waiting for a fish to appear.

If an osprey spots a fish, the bird dives toward the water. At the last instant before entering the water, the osprey swings its feet forward so the feet, with their big talons (claws), go into the water first and grab the fish. Spiny pads on the osprey's feet also help grip a slippery, squirming fish.

Successful or not, the osprey rises from the water and flies away, usually pausing in midair to shake off water. Only about one in four dives is successful, but when a fish is caught, the osprey will adjust its grip so the fish's head points forward in the same direction the

Where to see them

In the **Grand Canyon of the Yellowstone**, especially from Artist Point and Lookout Point, around **Yellowstone Lake**, along the **Madison River**, and along other large streams and lakes.

bird is flying. This makes the fish easier to carry.

An osprey takes the fish to a perch to eat or to its nest to feed its young. An osprey's nest is several feet across and made of sticks. It is usually on a rock pinnacle or the top of a tree. Many nests are used year after year.

Ospreys usually lay three eggs. Like bald eagles, ospreys were once declining in population because of the pesticide DDT, which the birds picked up from their food. The DDT caused their eggshells to be so thin that they broke when the adult birds tried to incubate them. Fortunately, the use of DDT was banned, and through protection and conservation, the population of ospreys is once again healthy.

Guess what?

The osprey is also called a "fish hawk" and feeds almost exclusively on fish.

☐ I saw an osprey!

Where?

When?

What was it doing?

20

Where to see them

Yellowstone Lake, the Yellowstone River in Hayden Valley, the Madison River, Lamar Valley, Blacktail Ponds, Pelican Creek Bridge, and Alum Creek.

Bald Eagle

(Haliaeetus leucocephalus)

The bald eagle is not really bald—its white head feathers just make it look that way. Only an adult bird has the white head and tail—it takes young birds nearly 5 years to develop this plumage; until then, they're mostly dark brown with a few white feathers here and there.

Eagles are "birds of prey." They mainly eat fish, but they also kill ducks and other animals, and eat carrion, or dead animals. Eagles often feed on carcasses of animals killed by wolves, after the wolves have left. The eagles tear off meat with their large yellow beaks.

It's not unusual for an eagle to ambush an osprey that is flying with a fish it has caught. The eagle swoops at the osprey and harasses it until the osprey drops the fish, which the eagle then grabs, sometimes in midair. Unlike an osprey, an eagle does not dive into the water for fish. Instead, it flies along and grabs fish that are floating or swimming at the water's surface.

Bald eagles stand nearly three feet tall. When extended, their wings are six to seven feet across.

In Yellowstone National Park, nesting bald eagles lay their eggs from late March to mid-April, usually when snow still covers the ground. While there are many nesting pairs of bald eagles here, the park is also important as a stopover for migrating eagles, especially in the fall.

Bald eagles are the emblem of the United States of America.

☐ I saw a bald eagle!

Where?

When?

What was it doing?

Guess What?

An eagle's nest can be thirteen feet tall and weigh nearly a ton. It is often used year after year.

American White Pelican

(Pelecanus erythrorhynchos)

If you see a large white bird on or near water, you might not be certain if it's a swan or a pelican, but if the bird has a huge orange-yellow bill, pelican it is. In flight, pelicans have prominent black wingtips, another good way to tell them from swans.

White pelicans are found along the oceans, but they also live and breed far inland. Other species of pelicans dive into the water for fish, but white pelicans work as a flock, swimming and sometimes walking to "herd" fish into shallow water where they scoop up the fish with their big bills. A soft pouch hanging from the bill expands to hold the fish, and the bird tips back its head to swallow the fish whole.

White pelicans nest in colonies, or rookeries. Because they nest on the ground, pelicans prefer places that can't be reached by predators such as foxes and coyotes. In Yellowstone National Park, the pelicans nest on small islands in Yellowstone Lake.

If you see a pelican with a strange bump on the top of its bill, there's nothing wrong with the bird—the bump appears in the spring during breeding season. It falls off later.

Yellowstone's white pelicans are migratory. They spend the winters in Mexico and southern California. When they fly, they flap their wings several times and then glide.

Guess what?
The average wingspan of the pelican ranges from 7 to 9 feet—that's almost as long as a small car.

☐ I saw a pelican!

Where?

When?

How many?

What were they doing?

22

Where to see them

Watch for dippers along any of the park's faster-moving streams, especially the **Gibbon, Gardner**, and **Madison rivers**, the **Yellowstone River** in its canyons, and the confluence of Soda Butte Creek and the **Lamar River**.

American Dipper

(Cinclus mexicanus)

The American dipper is fairly common in Yellowstone National Park, but don't bother searching for it in trees or meadows. Look for this bird along cold, fast streams and rapid rivers.

Dippers actually walk on the bottom of swift streams looking for their favorite aquatic insects to eat. Their strong toes give dippers a good grip on slippery rocks. To help it see clearly in fast-moving water, a dipper has built-in "goggles" in the form of an extra eyelid (called a nictitating membrane) on each eye. It also has a nostril flap that keeps water out of its nose.

Dippers are usually seen standing on streamside rocks or flying low over the water with rapid wing beats. When standing, it is usually dipping (bobbing) up and down; that's how it got its name.

Dippers are a little smaller than robins, plump, slate-gray, with short tails. If you watch one carefully you might see its eyes flash white—that's from tiny white feathers on its eyelids that you don't see until it blinks. But what this little bird lacks in color, it makes up for with its voice; its call is loud, bubbly, and musical.

Some people still refer to the bird by its old name, the water ouzel, and you may encounter many streams and waterfalls in the American West named Ouzel, after the bird.

Although many birds migrate to avoid Yellowstone's harsh winters, dippers stay year-round. They simply need rushing water that hasn't frozen over, and plenty of aquatic insects.

☐ I saw a dipper!

Where?

When?

What was it doing?

Guess what?
A group of American dippers is called a "ladle" of dippers.

23

Aspen

(Populus tremuloides)

Aspens are deciduous trees: they shed their leaves every fall and grow new leaves in the spring. Before the aspen leaves fall off, they change color to bright yellow-gold. Since most trees in Yellowstone are conifer trees that keep their green needles all year, aspen trees give Yellowstone a beautiful splash of color in the fall.

If you see an aspen up close, look carefully at its leaves and stems (but don't pick them). You'll discover how this tree got its name. The stems of most tree leaves are round, but the aspen's leaf stems are flattened, like a circle squashed into an oval. When the wind blows, the flattened stem causes the leaf to tremble and flutter, or "quake." See for yourself—blow gently on a leaf and watch it twist and turn. Aspen leaves are a little lighter in color on one side, making the fluttering more obvious.

Aspens produce seeds but most new trees grow as sprouts from the roots of an existing tree. Sometimes all the aspen trees in a grove have grown this way, so really, all the trees in that grove are parts of one single tree!

Aspen groves provide nesting habitat for many birds and food for many animals. Elk and moose often eat the leaves and small twigs on young aspens, and in winter they scrape off the bark of older trees with their teeth.

Fall colored aspens

Guess what?

New aspen trees sprout from the roots of an existing tree, so all it takes is one tree to eventually make a whole grove of aspen trees.

☐ I saw aspen trees!

Where?

When?

How many?

24

Where to see them

Lodgepole Pine

(Pinus contorta)

The lodgepole pine is the most abundant tree in Yellowstone National Park, lining the roads for miles and miles and making up about 80 percent of the park's trees. Most places in the park, there's probably a lodgepole pine within sight. To be sure, look closely at the tree's needles—the lodgepole is the only pine in Yellowstone with needles in bunches of two.

One reason lodgepole pines are so abundant is because they thrive after wildfires. Lodgepoles drop many pine cones and their seeds annually, but the top-most pine cones stay on the trees for years. These cones are sealed shut with sticky pine resin until the

heat from a wildfire melts the resin. Then these cones open up, spilling out their seeds. The fire burns out, but millions of lodgepole seeds lie on the ground and thousands of seeds successfully sprout into new trees. That's why lodgepole pines are among the first types of vegetation to grow after a forest fire.

Lodgepole pine forests provide food and shelter for many species. However, you may see large areas of pines that have turned red. These are trees that have been killed by a tiny insect called the mountain pine beetle. On the dead and dying trees, the green needles turn red before falling off. But many trees survive. Lodgepole pines are an important part of the park's ecosystem.

☐ I saw lodgepoles!

Where?

When?

How many?

Guess what?

Native Americans in the Rocky Mountains used, and still use, poles made from lodgepole pines for their tipis, or lodges, because the trees grow straight and tall with slender trunks. That's how this tree got its name.

Indian Paintbrush

(Castilleja species)

Where to see them

You can see Indian paintbrush throughout the park in meadows and near streams. Probably the best place to see little sunflowers is on Mount Washburn, but they are throughout the park on dry, open hillsides.

Little Sunflower

(Helianthella uniflora)

The Indian paintbrush, the state flower of Wyoming, got its name from a Native American legend. There are several variations of the story, but most say that a young boy named Little Gopher was too small to do what the other boys did, but Little Gopher had a different talent—he could paint. He had a vision that told him he would paint beautiful pictures of the tribe's warriors. Frustrated that the colors he had weren't bright enough, he asked the Great Spirit for help. The Great Spirit gave him paintbrushes with vivid colors. As Little Gopher used the brushes, he left them behind. The discarded brushes turned into flowers, the Indian paintbrushes.

Indian paintbrushes are about a foot tall and their flowers reach nearly halfway down the stems. They bloom from June through September and attract butterflies that drink their sweet nectar. There are many species of Indian paintbrush and they come in different colors, but in Yellowstone the most common color is red.

These yellow flowers are common in Yellowstone, and they often grow in huge numbers. Sometimes a hillside will look like it's painted yellow and blue: yellow from these flowers and blue from the lupines (see next page) growing with them.

While their most common name is "little sunflower," they are also called "one-flowered sunflower" because each plant stem only supports one flower. The flowers produce small seeds that birds love to eat.

Little sunflower; for a close-up of this flower, see page 5.

Guess What?

Wildflowers are an important part of Yellowstone's ecosystem. They provide food for various animals, from delicate butterflies to massive grizzly bears. Remember: Enjoy their beauty, but don't pick the flowers.

Indian paintbrush

☐ I saw wildflowers!

Where?

When?

What kind?

Lupine

(Lupinus species)

There are several species of lupine flowers in Yellowstone, most of them with blue or bluish purple flowers. Look for them growing in bunches on hillsides and mountains.

A lupine's flowers grow on all sides of a tall, straight stem. The height of the flower stem is a good clue that the plant is a lupine. Another good clue is the distinctive shape of a lupine's leaf. Several long, green leaflets (parts of the leaf) grow outwards from a common center, like a starburst. After a rain or heavy dew you can find drops of water trapped in the centers of the starbursts.

Lupine

Lupine is a legume, related to peas, beans, and peanuts. Legumes have seed pods that split open and special nodules (bumps) on their roots that help the plant take nitrogen out of the air and convert it to ammonia in the soil, which helps fertilize it.

Where to see them

You can see lupine throughout the park on hillsides, mountain meadows, and forest edges. Fireweed blooms from midsummer through fall. Look for large groups of these flowers along roads and forest edges, and in recently burned areas.

Fireweed

(Epilobium angustifolium)

Fireweed grows best on bare ground with few other plants growing nearby. In fact, fireweed is one of the first plants to grow after a forest fire, and that's how it got its name. It also grows where bare soil has been exposed, such as along roads, avalanche chutes, and eroding streambanks. Because it quickly establishes itself on bare ground before other plants start to grow, fireweed is often called a "pioneering species."

How does it get such a head start on other plants? Each fireweed stalk produces hundreds of tiny seeds that are carried long distances by the wind. When the seeds land on bare ground, they grow quickly. Fireweed is a tall plant, sometimes reaching six feet or more in height, and this height helps the seeds be blown farther by the wind.

Fireweed is often found in large colonies or clusters that are hard to miss. The flowers are bright pink or rose colored and cover the top foot or so of the stalk. The lowest flowers on the stalk bloom first. As summer progresses, flowers that are higher on the stalk bloom until finally the very tip-top flowers bloom.

Fireweed

27

Old Faithful Inn

Where to see it

Old Faithful historic area, which includes Upper Geyser Basin, the Old Faithful Visitor Center, and Old Faithful Geyser.

Old Faithful Inn is almost as famous as its geyser and has quite a history. It celebrated its 100th birthday in 2004, survived the 1988 fires thanks to a lot of hard work by firefighters, and withstood the 1959 Hebgen earthquake that rattled the building to its foundation. Through all its years, the inn has successfully hosted U.S. presidents, celebrities, and millions of visitors from around the world.

Old Faithful Inn was designed by Robert Reamer, a young architect who wanted the building to look as though it were part of its environment, part of nature—a design style that has come to be known as "parkitecture." Native materials were used to create the inn's rustic look—local stone for the foundation and fireplace, and lodgepole pine for the rafters and railings on the balconies on the upper floors.

The inn has 327 guest rooms, a large dining room, a large lobby (the dining room and lobby have huge fireplaces), a snack shop, gift shop, and other comforts. You can stand in the lobby and look 65 feet straight up to the roof or climb the log stairs to the next level, where you can go out onto the sun deck to watch Old Faithful erupt. If you have the time, take the free tour of the inn. Your guide might be Ruth Quinn (author of *Weaver of Dreams*, a book about the inn's architect), who will lead you through the halls and take you back in time.

Guess What?

The Old Faithful Inn is one of the few remaining log hotels in the United States.

☐ **I saw Old Faithful Inn!**

Where?

When?

What was it like?

Where to see it

Upper Geyser Basin, south of Madison Junction. You can watch Old Faithful from the boardwalk or from the upper deck at **Old Faithful Inn**. You can also watch it on the Internet at www.nps.gov/yell/photosmulti media/webcams.htm

Old Faithful Geyser

Old Faithful Geyser is the symbol of Yellowstone National Park, and its image is recognized by people all over the world. But nothing is quite as exciting as watching this geyser erupt in person, and each year millions of people do just that.

Geysers are found in volcanic areas. In Yellowstone, you're in a caldera, the center of a volcano, but the molten lava, or magma, is underground. The heat from the magna, combined with ground water, creates the park's hot springs, geysers, and other thermal features.

Beneath the surface of a hot spring are various cracks and openings that allow the ground water to reach the surface. Geysers are like hot springs except geysers have narrow cracks or openings beneath them. These narrow openings make it harder for the hot water and steam to rise to the surface, but eventually so much pressure builds up that the water and steam squeezes through the narrow cracks and shoots to the surface, erupting as a geyser.

Old Faithful Geyser was named because its eruptions were regular or "faithful." It still is, but the time between eruptions does vary, depending on the length of the previous eruption. After a short eruption Old Faithful doesn't need as much time to get ready for the next show, perhaps only an hour. After a longer eruption, it needs more time, maybe 90 minutes, to recharge before it blows again. Old Faithful has been studied so much, and its eruptions are so regular, that it is the most predictable geyser on earth. Estimated eruption times are posted on clocks in Old Faithful Inn and visitor centers.

When it does erupt, Old Faithful shoots thousands of gallons of water into the air. The water soars from 106 to more than to 180 feet above the ground, and the eruption lasts from two to five minutes. Be sure to see it.

☐ I saw Old Faithful Geyser!

Where?

When?

What was it like?

Guess What?

Old Faithful Geyser isn't the largest geyser in Yellowstone, but it is the most regular. Steamboat Geyser is the tallest, but is not dependable—it may not erupt for many years.

29

Midway Geyser Basin

Where to see it

About halfway (midway, get it?)
between **Old Faithful** and
Madison Junction.

You could spend an entire day exploring the thermal areas between Madison and Old Faithful, including Lower Geyser Basin, Midway Geyser Basin, and Upper Geyser Basin. Within these basins are Fountain Paint Pot Trail and Firehole Lake Drive, both with many thermal features.

Grand Prismatic Spring is in Midway Geyser Basin, and it is the largest hot spring in the United States. Whether because of its size, its beautiful color, or its location near the road, it is one of the most visited and photographed hot springs in Yellowstone. Morning

Glory Pool is another popular and beautiful hot spring but you need to walk about 1.5 miles (one way) to see it.

Along Firehole Lake Drive is Great Fountain Geyser, whose bursts can last nearly an hour. Its eruptions are usually about 100 feet high but if you're lucky you might see 200-foot bursts. Unfortunately, Great Fountain Geyser is not as predictable as Old Faithful; you might have to wait several hours to see Great Fountain's plume because it only erupts twice a day.

Firehole River

Thermal water draining
into the Firehole River

Guess What?

Several hot springs and geysers spill directly into the Firehole River, but the river is still cold enough to have trout.

Excelsior Geyser crater

30

Grand Prismatic Spring

☐ I Saw Midway Geyser Basin!

Where?

When?

What was it like?

Grand Pristmatic Spring

West Thumb Geyser Basin

Where to see it
On the west side of **Yellowstone Lake. Grant Village** is located here.

At the eastern edge of Yellowstone Lake is West Thumb Geyser Basin, a thermal area of mud pots, hot springs, and geysers. West Thumb is an unusual area because it is a caldera within a caldera. A caldera is the center of a volcano that has collapsed; most of Yellowstone National Park is within a caldera that formed hundreds of thousands of years ago.

As you walk through the West Thumb Geyser Basin, you might notice a strange smell, usually described as "rotten eggs." This is hydrogen sulfide, a gas that mixes with oxygen in the water before finding its way to the surface.

See the different colors in the hot pools? Most of the colors are actually collections of tiny organisms called thermophiles. Each species is a different color, and each prefers a different water temperature. West Thumb contains one of the deeper hot springs in Yellowstone: it's 53-feet-deep Abyss Pool, a blue-and-green spring that last erupted in 1992.

Abyss Pool

Fishing Cone, a thermal feature near the shore of Yellowstone Lake

Guess What?
West Thumb got its name because to early visitors Yellowstone Lake appeared shaped like a hand, with this bay being the "Thumb."

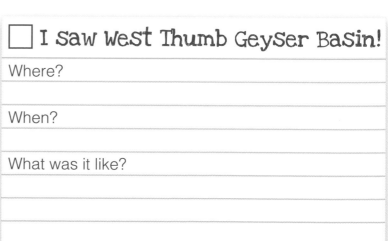

☐ **I saw West Thumb Geyser Basin!**

Where?

When?

What was it like?

32

Where to see it

From the road between **West Thumb** and **Fishing Bridge**, **Lake Visitor Center** and from shoreline trails.

Yellowstone Lake is one of the great sights in Yellowstone National Park. It is *big* (about 20 miles long and 14 miles wide), *deep* (410 feet at its deepest spot, about as deep as a 40-story building is tall), and *cold* (even during the summer the lake's water temperature is only between 40 and 50 degrees).

Some people think Yellowstone Lake is the source of the Yellowstone River, but the river actually begins in northwestern Wyoming and enters Yellowstone Lake at the Southeast Arm, a remote part of the lake that can be reached only by trail, canoe, or kayak.

The river leaves the lake at Fishing Bridge and flows through the park into Montana.

Yellowstone Lake is 7,733 feet above sea level. At this elevation, the long, cold winters keep the lake frozen over until late May or early June, but the lake is still home to many fish species, especially the Yellowstone cutthroat trout. A good place to watch the trout is from Fishing Bridge at the lake's outlet.

There's plenty of other wildlife around the lake, such as bald eagles, ospreys, moose, and sometimes bears. You can take a tour boat and find out about the lake's Native American and early explorer history as well as its plants and animals.

Yellowstone Lake

☐ I saw Yellowstone Lake!

Where?

When?

What was it like?

Guess what?

There are active hot springs on the bottom of Yellowstone Lake. In some spots the water coming out of the thermal vents can be close to boiling, even though the deep lake water may be close to freezing.

Grand Canyon

of the Yellowstone

Look into the Grand Canyon of the Yellowstone River and you will see how Yellowstone National Park got its name—the sandstone rock cliffs are yellow. You will also see the two spectacular falls of the Yellowstone River.

Lower Falls

On the South Rim of the canyon is Artist Point, one of the most photographed views in Yellowstone. From several overlook platforms you can see the Upper and Lower falls. When the snow melts in the spring, there might be more than 60,000 gallons of water flowing over the falls every second!

Grand Canyon of the Yellowstone

If you take Uncle Tom's Trail to the bottom of the canyon, you will feel the spray of the falls and feel the ground tremble from the force of all that water thundering over the rocks.

Trails from the North Rim take you to Lower Falls, the tallest waterfall in Yellowstone at 308 feet high.

Guess what?

At the Canyon Visitor Education Center there is a mysterious 9,000-pound rock that floats on water! Stop by the center to find out the rock's secret.

☐ **I saw the Grand Canyon of the Yellowstone!**

Where?

When?

What was it like?

Where to see it

Mammoth is in the northwestern part of Yellowstone, 5 miles from **Gardiner**. The Albright Visitor Center is open 365 days a year.

Mammoth Hot Springs

Mammoth Hot Springs and Terraces are a colorful, ever-changing collection of hot pools and rocky formations in Yellowstone National Park. The hot water contains dissolved limestone. As the water flows out of the ground, chemical changes take place and some of the dissolved limestone becomes the mineral travertine. Travertine is deposited as hard rock, and this process builds the pools and terraces. Sometimes so much travertine is formed that it spreads over the boardwalks that allow visitors to walk around the hot springs. Then the boardwalks have to be moved.

In the park's early days, no one was here to protect it from vandals who destroyed thermal features, killed the park's wildlife, and even bathed in the hot springs. For a time the U.S. Army managed the park, and Fort Yellowstone was established at Mammoth. You can take a walking tour of the fort area and see the guardhouse (jail), blacksmith shop, barracks, stables, and more. Guidebooks are available at the Albright Visitor Center.

Mammoth terraces

☐ I Saw Mammoth!

Where?

When?

What was it like?

Liberty Cone

Guess What?
Mammoth was named for the large sizes of the hot springs and thermal formations there.

Where to see them

You can see the 45th Parallel between the North Entrance and Mammoth in **Gardner Canyon**. Watch for the tour buses on any of the park's roads. If you pass one, be sure to wave to the passengers and driver.

The 45th Parallel sign in Yellowstone National Park tells you that you are halfway between the equator and the North Pole. In 2008, with global positioning systems and satellite imaging, scientists discovered the sign was actually off by a mile, so they moved it. Now it's about 1,000 feet from the true position of the 45th Parallel, as close as the sign could be placed without disturbing any land. As it turns out, moving the sign was good for visitor safety too. People would pull over to have their pictures taken with the sign, which was right along the road. In the new location there is plenty of space to have a picture taken that proves you are halfway between the equator and the North Pole.

In the 1930s the long, yellow, low-slung buses were the only way groups of tourists could get around the park. The men who drove them were called "gear-jammers" because of all the shifting or "jamming" of engine gears they did as they navigated steep hills. The vehicles didn't have power steering or power brakes and were difficult to maneuver around the hard turns, or to stop quickly for animals in the road. The old Ford buses were made specifically for Yellowstone, but when newer cars and buses arrived on the scene, the special yellow buses faded away with disuse. In 2007 they were refurbished and given new life on the park roads. Take one for a scenic ride and hear a guided tour from the driver.

Guess what?

Although the town of Gardiner and the Gardner River are spelled differently, both are correct. Years ago, an error in speaking the name was written down both ways, and they stuck.

☐ I saw the 45th Parallel!

☐ I saw a tour bus!

Where?

When?

What was it like?

where to see it

In **Gardiner**, just west of the Yellowstone Association store and next to the high school football field.

Roosevelt Arch

In the early 1900s, the few roads leading to Yellowstone National Park were in awful condition, and people found it difficult to get to the park. When the Northern Pacific Railway built a depot at Gardiner, tourism picked up slightly because visitors could take the train to the park's entrance. From the depot, stagecoaches transported visitors into the park. But the entrance to this "wonderland" still looked kind of bleak, so Hiram Chittenden, an officer in the Army Corps of Engineers in charge of park roads, suggested an arch at the park's first entrance.

The massive stone structure was officially dedicated in 1903 with a ceremony attended by thousands of people. U.S. President Theodore Roosevelt, who was vacationing in Yellowstone at the time, was asked to lay the cornerstone for the arch, which was then named after him.

The arch bears three inscriptions. The main inscription reads: "For the Benefit and Enjoyment of the People," which is what a national park is meant to be. On the east tower are the words "Yellowstone National Park," and on the west tower, "Created by an act of Congress March 3d, 1872."

As roads continued to be built and people could afford cars, more entrances to Yellowstone were created. Fewer people traveled by train and the depot at Gardiner eventually closed, but the arch still stands and greets visitors from all over the world.

□ I saw the Roosevelt Arch!

Where?

When?

What was it like?

Guess what?

More park visitors have their photos taken at the Roosevelt Arch than any other place except Old Faithful.

Park Programs

Junior Ranger

If you're between 5 and 12 years old you can become a Junior Ranger. The program is offered by the National Park Service and is available in more than 200 of America's national parks. All it takes to get started is the free "Yellowstone's Nature" activity booklet that you can get at any visitor center.

Complete the booklet activities and present it to a ranger, who will make sure you completed it correctly and award you with an official sew-on ranger patch.

Campfire talk

Young Scientist

You might look closely at insects, you might use a stopwatch to time Old Faithful or another geyser's eruption, or you might even test some of the thermal waters' temperatures as part of the Young Scientist program, open to all kids ages 5 and up. Who knows, you may even discover a new species of plant or animal, but even if you don't you'll learn more than the average park visitor and come away from the program with that knowledge and a sew-on patch or keychain. For a few dollars you can purchase the booklet you need to get you started, then follow the directions until you have completed all the activities. Young Scientist program booklets are available at Canyon and Old Faithful visitor education centers.

Ranger-led Programs

You can see most if not all of Yellowstone from your vehicle, and the park's interpretive signs are top-notch, but for learning behind-the-scenes, little-known facts, you can't beat a ranger-led program. These programs are conducted all year throughout the park at nearly every major feature: you may watch the stars, learn about wolves, discover geysers, or snowshoe—the list is impressive. Some programs involve walks and gentle hikes; others are held in the campground amphitheaters. Schedules are posted at all visitor centers; in the park newspaper, which you receive when you enter the park; and online at www.nps.gov.

Guess What?

Yellowstone National Park has an entire museum dedicated to national park rangers. It is housed in the restored log Norris Soldier Station near the entrance to the Norris Campground.

More Things I Saw Checklist

Yellowstone National Park has 67 mammal species, 322 recorded bird species, more than a thousand plant species, thousands of thermal features, and countless special places—so you can't see *everything* in one trip. But in addition to the items already described, here is a list of other common things in the park. Check off what you see, and good luck!

Pronghorn antelope

Wildlife

- [ ] Badger
- [ ] Beaver
- [ ] Golden-mantled ground squirrel
- [ ] Moose
- [ ] Mountain goat
- [ ] Pika
- [ ] Porcupine
- [ ] Pronghorn antelope
- [ ] Red fox
- [ ] River otter
- [ ] Yellowstone cutthroat trout

Golden-mantled ground squirrel

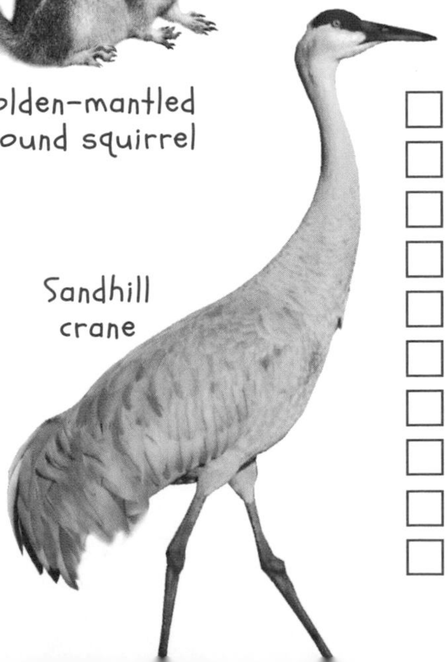

Sandhill crane

Birds

- [ ] Canada goose
- [ ] Chickadee
- [ ] Clark's nutcracker
- [ ] Dark-eyed junco
- [ ] Gray jay
- [ ] Great blue heron
- [ ] Mountain bluebird
- [ ] Sandhill crane
- [ ] Steller's jay
- [ ] Trumpeter swan

Electric Peak

Places

- [ ] Electric Peak
- [ ] Gibbon Falls
- [ ] Lake Hotel
- [ ] Lewis Lake
- [ ] Mount Washburn
- [ ] Museum of the National Park Ranger
- [ ] Sheepeater Cliffs
- [ ] Tower Falls
- [ ] Upper Falls

Geysers and Thermal Features

- [ ] Artists Paintpots
- [ ] Beehive Geyser
- [ ] Black Pool
- [ ] Castle Geyser
- [ ] Morning Glory Pool
- [ ] Norris Geyser Basin
- [ ] Roaring Mountain
- [ ] Soda Butte

Beehive Geyser

Dedication
To Woody

Acknowledgments
A sincere thank you to John Johanek, Beth Kaeding, Lynn Kaeding, Jan Laye, Jack Gilchrist, Ilona Popper, Doug Smith, Elsa Thompson and the *Bird Watcher's Digest* staff, Jennifer Whipple, and Chris Wonderly, who contributed valuable information to this checklist. A special thanks to the good folks at Riverbend Publishing for taking on the project and seeing it to publication.

About the Author
Since 1992 Durrae Johanek has lived in Bozeman, Montana. She graduated from Kutztown University of Pennsylvania with a degree in English, which she has put to good use ever since, first in the public relations department at ALPO Petfoods, then for more than 25 years as a freelance editor that included nearly a decade as editorial consultant to *Bird Watcher's Digest* magazine. *What I Saw in Yellowstone* is Durrae's fourth book. She also wrote *The Yellowstone National Park Cookbook* and coauthored with her husband, John, *Montana Behind the Scenes* and *Montana Folks*. When not struggling with the written word, she enjoys birding, quilting, spinning, and exploring nature with John as often as possible.

What I Saw in Yellowstone
Text © 2012 by Durrae Johanek
Photographs © by Christopher Cauble, www.caublephotography.com
Published by Riverbend Publishing, Helena, Montana

Design by Sarah Cauble, www.sarahcauble.com

ISBN 13: 978-1-60639-035-1

Printed in the United States of America

11 12 13 14 15 VP 22 21 20 19

Riverbend Publishing
P.O. Box 5833
Helena, MT 59604
1-866-787-2363
www.riverbendpublishing.com